Diseases and Disorders

Epilepsy

Titles in the Diseases and Disorders series include:

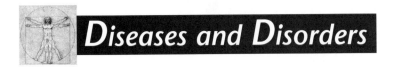

Epilepsy

by Gregory Goodfellow

Library of Congress Cataloging-in-Publication Data
Goodfellow, Greg.
   Epilepsy / by Greg Goodfellow.
      p. cm. — (Diseases and disorders series)
   Includes bibliographical references and index.
   Summary: Discusses the causes, diagnosis, and treatment of epilepsy, the types of seizures, and the challenges of living with the disease.
      ISBN 1-56006-701-2 (lib.: alk. paper)
   1. Epilepsy—Juvenile literature. [1. Epilepsy. 2. Diseases.] I. Title. II. Series.
RC372.2.G66   2001
616.8'53—dc21   00-008657

Copyright © 2001 by Lucent Books, Inc.
P.O. Box 289011
San Diego, CA 92198-9011
Printed in the U.S.A.

Table of Contents

"The Most Difficult Puzzles Ever Devised"

CHARLES BEST, ONE of the pioneers in the search for a cure for diabetes, once explained what it is about medical research that intrigued him so. "It's not just the gratification of knowing one is helping people," he confided, "although that probably is a more heroic and selfless motivation. Those feelings may enter in, but truly, what I find best is the feeling of going toe to toe with nature, of trying to solve the most difficult puzzles ever devised. The answers are there somewhere, those keys that will solve the puzzle and make the patient well. But how will those keys be found?"

Since the dawn of civilization, nothing has so puzzled people— and often frightened them, as well—as the onset of illness in a body or mind that had seemed healthy before. A seizure, the inability of a heart to pump, the sudden deterioration of muscle tone in a small child—being unable to reverse such conditions or even to understand why they occur was unspeakably frustrating to healers. Even before there were names for such conditions, even before they were understood at all, each was a reminder of how complex the human body was, and how vulnerable.

While our grappling with understanding diseases has been frustrating at times, it has also provided some of humankind's most heroic accomplishments. Alexander Fleming's accidental discovery in 1928 of a mold that could be turned into penicillin

6

has resulted in the saving of untold millions of lives. The isolation of the enzyme insulin has reversed what was once a death sentence for anyone with diabetes. There have been great strides in combating conditions for which there is not yet a cure, too. Medicines can help AIDS patients live longer, diagnostic tools such as mammography and ultrasounds can help doctors find tumors while they are treatable, and laser surgery techniques have made the most intricate, minute operations routine.

This "toe-to-toe" competition with diseases and disorders is even more remarkable when seen in a historical continuum. An astonishing amount of progress has been made in a very short time. Just two hundred years ago, the existence of germs as a cause of some diseases was unknown. In fact, it was less than 150 years ago that a British surgeon named Joseph Lister had difficulty persuading his fellow doctors that washing their hands before delivering a baby might increase the chances of a healthy delivery (especially if they had just attended to a diseased patient)!

Each book in Lucent's *Diseases and Disorders* series explores a disease or disorder and the knowledge that has been accumulated (or discarded) by doctors through the years. Each book also examines the tools used for pinpointing a diagnosis, as well as the various means that are used to treat or cure a disease. Finally, new ideas are presented—techniques or medicines that may be on the horizon.

Frustration and disappointment are still part of medicine, for not every disease or condition can be cured or prevented. But the limitations of knowledge are being pushed outward constantly; the "most difficult puzzles ever devised" are finding challengers every day.

A Temporary Loss of Control

I think people with epilepsy know best how amazing the brain is. Only we [those with epilepsy] know how fragile it is, yet how powerfully strong it is at the same time. Everybody's seen pictures of the brain, it really looks . . . like nothing's happening inside of it. . . . Most people just think of it as "there." But if you have epilepsy you can't ignore what the brain hides or what it's always doing, because at any moment your world could get turned upside down because of some tiny little problem somewhere in your brain. . . . If you're stressing out during a math exam or . . . just sitting there watching cartoons, your brain is always in control. Only people with epilepsy know what it's like for your brain to suddenly lose control . . . and you can't compare the feeling to anything else.[1]

—Nigel,* age seventeen

THE HUMAN BRAIN differs from all of the other organs in the body because at every moment it is coordinating and controlling behavior, from every movement of the toes to the plots of nightly dreams. The brain can do these things because it is the only organ that employs its own form of communication. It creates endless amounts of specific messages every second of the day, and then it constantly sends this information to all of the other body parts. In this way, the brain is able to lead the entire body—to control all movement and to shape all thought and emotion.

* All of the names of patients and their families have been changed to protect their privacy.

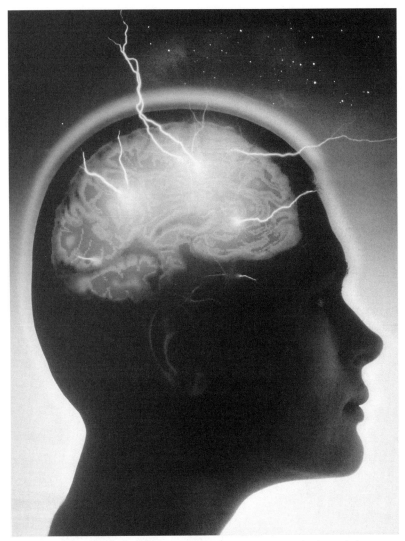

A computerized image depicts a cross-section of a human brain emitting electro-chemical charges. This communication in the brain mediates diverse functions including thought, movement, and breathing.

Epilepsy is a medical disorder in which the way that the brain communicates gets momentarily mixed up. For just a few moments, some or all of the brain's messages get confused and the wrong information gets sent out. The body then reacts accordingly, and these momentary mix-ups result in a sudden surge of uncontrollable, abnormal behavior. For instance, if an incorrect message is sent to an arm, telling it to jerk at random, the arm will jerk. If an incorrect message is created to make a person feel sad, he or she will feel that way, even in a happy situation. These recurring interruptions define epilepsy and usually occur together, producing many different behavioral alterations at a time, not just one jerking arm or one strange emotion.

Therefore, as Nigel explains, what people with epilepsy experience over and over is a temporary loss of control over how they act and feel. It is a feeling unlike any other, both frightening and hard to understand. However, such feelings are only temporary. In between these short episodes, nearly all of the 40 million people with epilepsy worldwide enjoy fulfilled, normal lives, and their brains function just like anybody else's.

A woman with epilepsy plays with her seizure-alert dog, which has been trained to recognize symptoms of his owner's upcoming seizures and give a warning bark before their onset.

They can live this way because scientists have discovered incredible methods to both diagnose and treat the disorder. Furthermore, individuals with epilepsy remain optimistic that the condition's symptoms may soon be things of the past as researchers and doctors uncover new and exciting ways to treat and perhaps one day cure the disorder known as epilepsy.

Chapter 1

What Is Epilepsy?

THE WORD EPILEPSY comes from an ancient Greek word that means to grab, seize, or attack. Today, *epilepsy* describes a disorder in which sudden bursts sometimes occur in the electricity that is present within the brain and that allows the brain to function properly. These short disturbances in the brain's fragile electrical balance are called seizures, and when an individual experiences two or more of them at random, he or she is considered to have epilepsy. Depending on where in the brain they occur, seizures can momentarily alter an individual's behavior in many different ways. In essence, that person is suddenly seized or grabbed by a shift in behavior that he or she cannot control. A

Emily, a middle-school student, rests with her dog after having a seizure at her school.

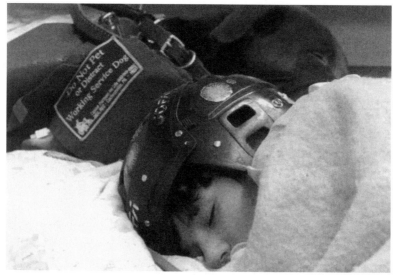

seizure can mean a variety of startling displays, from a few moments of blank staring or confused babbling to an attack of violent muscle spasms or total loss of consciousness.

Epilepsy and epileptic seizures are much more common than most people think, affecting more than 40 million people worldwide and nearly 3 million individuals in the United States alone. Epilepsy is never contagious, is rarely life threatening, and is usually treatable with medication.

Understanding epilepsy begins with the awareness of one simple fact: Epilepsy is not a disease that causes seizures. A single seizure can strike anyone under certain circumstances, such as during an allergic reaction to a drug or after a serious head injury. Instead, epilepsy is simply the abnormal condition in which an individual's brain has the tendency to suffer from repeated seizures under any circumstances.

What Causes Epilepsy?

Epilepsy is a disorder for which many possible causes have been determined, yet the cause behind most cases still remains a mystery. As it stands today, 70 percent of all cases of epilepsy are idiopathic, meaning that no cause for them can be pinpointed. The other 30 percent are cases of symptomatic epilepsy, for which a definite cause is known.

The mystery of idiopathic epilepsy can be very frustrating to both patients and doctors. In such cases, no other abnormality in the structure or function of the brain exists to explain the disorder. Although these cases of epilepsy are a long-standing mystery, it is becoming more and more clear that genetics may be a cause of idiopathic epilepsy. This means that the disorder may be handed down through generations, much in the same way that hair or eye color is.

A large majority of patients with idiopathic epilepsy come from families with a history of epilepsy. A closer look at these families often reveals repeated patterns in the way that epilepsy is passed on through generations. According to the Epilepsy Foundation of America, the likelihood of one parent with epilepsy passing the disorder on to a child is 6 percent, and that figure jumps to 12 percent if both parents have epilepsy. The influence of genetics on epilepsy is a very exciting topic. It may help solve an intriguing mystery, and for that reason, it has recently become the focus of considerable research.

Unlike with idiopathic epilepsy, there are many known causes of symptomatic epilepsy. Examples include external injury, such as severe head trauma received during an auto accident; the presence of certain diseases or medical conditions, such as AIDS or an infection of the blood surrounding the brain; and developmental problems, such as the malformation of the brain during a traumatic childbirth. All of these unfortunate circumstances can result in epilepsy.

Who Has Epilepsy?

Although scientists can't be sure of the causes behind most cases of epilepsy, they do know one thing: Epilepsy affects all types of people. Each day, 150,000 people are diagnosed with epilepsy, and in this group are both men and women, individuals of all races and age groups, and people from all parts of the world. However, although it can strike anyone, epilepsy does show up among certain groups much more frequently than others. For reasons that are not well understood, males are diagnosed with epilepsy at a higher rate than females. And epilepsy is most common among two age groups: those under the age of twenty and those over the age of sixty-five.

Epilepsy is often considered a condition of childhood due to patterns that have always been present among cases of idiopathic epilepsy: The disorder usually presents itself at a young age and then disappears upon early adulthood. The vast majority of patients with idiopathic epilepsy experience their first seizure sometime between the ages of five and nineteen. In fact, when the statistics for both idiopathic and symptomatic epilepsy are combined, they show a strong slant toward childhood: Seventy-five percent of all cases of epilepsy begin before the age of eighteen. In addition, people who are afflicted with epilepsy at a young age have a 68 to 93 percent chance of growing out of the disorder naturally, within twenty years after it is diagnosed.

Therefore, many of these individuals live their adult lives without the disorder.

Second only to children, senior citizens are more susceptible to epilepsy than other adults because of the general weakness and vulnerability that result from aging. Dangerous medical events and conditions that can cause epilepsy are far more frequent after the age of sixty-five. One such condition is a stroke, an event in which blood supply is cut off from part of the brain. Seniors who have experienced a stroke are more likely to develop epilepsy than people who have never had one. Researchers speculate that conditions like these take a greater toll on the brain and nervous system of an older individual, and for that reason, they have a greater chance of leading to epilepsy.

Regardless of what conditions have led to epilepsy or the characteristics of the person who has the disorder, the event that defines epilepsy—the seizure—always has similar properties. A look into the structure and function of the brain reveals these properties.

Seizures from the Inside

The first thing doctors investigate when trying to understand seizures is neurons. Neurons are cells that make up every human brain and are specialized for electrical communication. They have branchlike extensions, called axons, that connect them to one another and act as pathways for electrical impulses. In every brain, the electrical impulses that neurons fire between one another convey one of only two different messages. They either communicate to the neuron on the receiving end to fire again, thus continuing the chain of electrical communication, or they do the opposite, ending the chain. In the working brain, trillions of these electrical messages flow continuously between billions of interconnected neurons. The result is a network of coordinated and balanced electrical activity that controls all aspects of human behavior.

During a seizure, one group of neurons suddenly misfires its impulses, causing a chain reaction of incorrect interaction among the cells. In a sense, the brain's electricity is momentarily short-circuited. This synchronized surge of electrical miscommunication spreads quickly throughout either one part or the entire

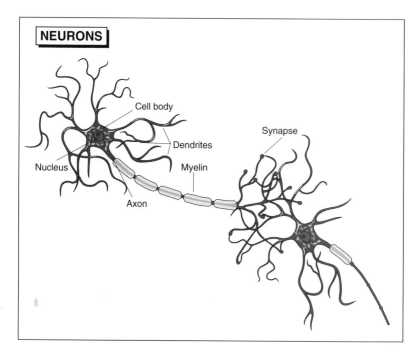

NEURONS

Cell body

Synapse

Dendrites

Nucleus

Myelin

Axon

brain. An article in *New Scientist* magazine says that "Epileptic fits [seizures] are sparked by brain cells talking to each other faster than usual. . . . When certain brain cells fire they somehow persuade others to do the same."[2]

Messages to the Body

This electrical miscommunication between cells always begins in the brain. However, it does not end there. There is a group of neurons that connects the brain to the rest of the body. These neurons transfer the impulses to other areas of the body, allowing the brain to control the movement and motion of other body parts. Such neurons have much longer axons, which extend downward from the brain to the body, and these axons act as the electrical wiring on which the electrical impulses travel. Therefore, the electrical surge of a seizure can quickly spread from the brain to another part of the body, sending that body part an incorrect message. Such a message results in the uncontrollable muscle movement that often characterizes seizures. Depending on where in the brain it takes place, a seizure can affect just one body part or it can affect the entire body. This is because different areas of the brain control different areas of the body.

Two Groups of Seizures

There are two factors that shape the effect that seizures have on the individual they strike: namely, where in the brain the seizure takes place and how far throughout the brain it spreads. Although the World Health Organization recognizes a total of nearly forty types of seizures, doctors who specialize in the brain and its function, called neurologists, split all seizures into two major groups based on these factors. These two groups are partial seizures and generalized seizures. Partial seizures occur in a specific area of the brain and remain in that area for their entire duration. Generalized seizures, on the other hand, spread very quickly throughout the entire brain. A closer look at these two groups of seizures shows the many ways in which seizures can alter the behavior of the individuals they strike.

Partial Seizures

Partial seizures are the most common type of seizure. They can take place anywhere in the brain. Yet because they affect only a specific area of the brain, they often present themselves very subtly and may even go unnoticed. Depending on where in the brain they take place, the mixed-up messages created by partial seizures spread only to specific areas of the body and affect only specific behaviors. For example, a partial seizure that occurs in the area of the brain that controls facial muscles will result only in an uncontrolled twitching of the mouth, nose, eyes, or other facial features. Similarly, a partial seizure that is focused in the section of the brain that monitors the sense of smell could result in an individual who is suddenly overcome by a familiar scent, such as lavender or vanilla. Either way, confused electrical signals result in abnormal behavior.

The following is twenty-five-year-old Steven's description of the partial seizures he often experiences. His seizures are an example of a common type of partial seizure, which takes place in the area of the brain controlling memory and spoken language skills. Steven's confusion and out-of-place feeling are very common results of seizures that occur in an area of the brain that controls some aspect of mental behavior. Steven says,

> Each one starts with the feeling of dropping quickly on a roller coaster. Then, whatever I happen to be looking at when the seizure starts all of the sudden feels like a very significant object from my past, usually having to do with some stressful family event. . . . I start to get confused about where I am. . . . Then I lose my ability to put a sentence together and I black out for a few moments. I usually sit quietly . . . afterward. . . . Most of the time no one can tell what happened.[3]

Generalized Seizures

Generalized seizures affect a much larger area of the brain than partial seizures do. Therefore, they have a greater chance of altering many more aspects of an individual's behavior. This means that they are usually much more dramatic. In fact, the seizure most often associated with epilepsy is a type of generalized seizure that can be very frightening to those who witness it. The convulsion, as it is commonly known, involves a total loss of muscle control in which the individual's entire body stiffens and shakes violently before becoming limp and falling to the floor. These seizures can also result in a loss of consciousness and an increase in heart rate and blood pressure. Here, Elana describes the generalized seizure that struck her boyfriend, Robert, one morning in a coffee shop:

> What caught my attention this time was the noise the legs of his chair started making. . . . I looked up from my book and saw that his neck was flung back and his arms were shot downward all stiff. Then his body suddenly loosened up and his right side began shaking. . . . The people sitting behind us jumped up when Robert dropped to the floor and began asking me what they should do . . . and because he fell to the right his whole right side was covered in dust from writhing on the floor. Strangely, the girl at the counter didn't move until he started drooling . . . then she ran over in tears.[4]

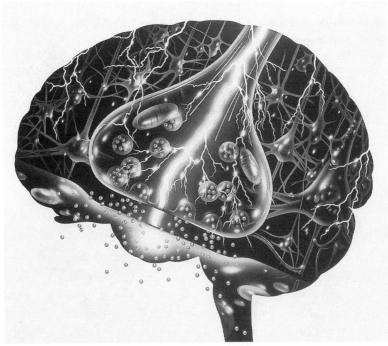

This abstract artwork, based on a patient's description of what an epileptic seizure feels like, shows lightning against a background of nerve cells inside a human brain.

This is only one example of the many types of generalized seizures. Furthermore, both generalized and partial seizures present themselves in a variety of ways and become very personal, individualized events for each person who experiences them.

The Effects of Epilepsy

In spite of these difficulties, most people with epilepsy lead healthy, outwardly normal lives. Famous statesmen such as Napoléon, Julius Caesar, and Peter the Great had the disorder. So did artists like Vincent van Gogh and scientists such as Alfred Nobel, after whom the Nobel Prize is named. These figures stand as proof that epilepsy is not a disabling disorder and that it does not have to negatively shape an individual's entire lifestyle. This is certainly true today, when nearly 80 percent of people are able to control their epilepsy with some form of modern treatment

Famous statesmen Julius Caesar, Peter the Great, and Napoléon (pictured) all lived with epilepsy and are testament to the fact that epilepsy is not a disabling disorder.

therapy. However, the disorder can also have negative effects, including both behavioral and emotional problems. And as a general rule, the effects are divided by age. Children with epilepsy often encounter one set of obstacles while adults usually face another.

Epilepsy in Children

All children struggle with the fears and confusion that accompany constant learning, growth, and new experiences. Epilepsy, however, has a tendency to multiply these basic barriers. Common issues such as educational problems, day-to-day fears of the unknown, and low self-esteem are often highlighted and increased in the lives of kids who have this disorder.

Children with epilepsy are slightly more prone to learning disabilities, behavioral problems, and emotional upset than other children are. Research has shown that frequent seizures, and the loss of attention that usually accompanies them, can affect a child's overall attention span and memory. This makes necessary learning and educational tools, such as reading and writing, more difficult to master. In addition, children who experience frequent seizures are often absent from school more often than other students.

It is also not uncommon for children with epilepsy to develop behavioral and emotional problems. Sometimes these problems are caused by the general embarrassment and frustration associated with seizures. However, they can also result from the constant fear of not knowing when a seizure will strike. No treatment for epilepsy provides 100 percent control of seizures, and because seizures tend to occur very suddenly and at random

A teacher's aide helps a young student with epilepsy with math work assigned in her mainstream class.

times, the nagging stress of a seizure happening at an embarrassing moment is difficult for many children with epilepsy to escape.

Finally, children with epilepsy have an increased risk of poor self-esteem and depression. A seizure in school may result in bullying or teasing, which may continue for a long period. Such constant harassment is extremely difficult for any child; to children already grappling with a seizure disorder, it is almost unbearable. Children with epilepsy often feel less adequate than siblings and peers, and harsh treatment only worsens this.

Epilepsy in Adults

Although similar behavioral and emotional issues can also affect adults with epilepsy, older individuals with the disorder generally tend to face a different set of obstacles. Most common is a restricted sense of independence. Most states will not issue a driver's license to someone with epilepsy unless that person can prove that she or he has been seizure-free for a certain length of time (in most states, for at least six months to one year). For an adult with the busy schedule created by career and family, this can cause constant problems.

In addition, adults with epilepsy often find that their employment opportunities are restricted or that they receive unfair treatment on the job. In fact, 25 percent of adults with epilepsy are unemployed, a much higher rate than the rest of the population's. And many people with epilepsy feel that other people's misconceptions about the disorder are what lead to unfair treatment on the job. "I've had to miss a couple of days of work this year because of seizures," forty-six-year-old Mark explains, "and both times I felt like I had to lie about why I was gone. It just seems that the moment people you work with find out about your epilepsy, they trust you less as a fellow employee."[5] For adults and children, it is clear that the reactions of others to epilepsy can affect their lives as much as the disorder itself can.

Is Epilepsy Life Threatening?

Epilepsy can cause death, but only very rarely. There are, however, two life-threatening conditions that people with epilepsy

Most states require those with epilepsy to prove that they have been seizure-free for a certain length of time before they are allowed a driver's license.

are at a greater risk of experiencing than the general population. These two circumstances are *status epilepticus* and death resulting from a high-risk activity.

Status epilepticus is a very severe condition in which a person either has an extremely prolonged seizure or has a group of quickly repeating seizures and does not regain consciousness between each one. Doctors disagree on the amount of time that should pass during a prolonged seizure before a person is diagnosed with *status epilepticus;* some say five minutes while others say ten or even thirty minutes. In any case, the condition can grab hold of the body's most vital functions until death occurs. Of the nearly 3 million people who have epilepsy in the United States, 100,000 report experiencing *status epilepticus* each year. About half of those cases interrupt normal heart and lung function so severely that they result in death.

The other life-threatening situation that those with epilepsy risk encountering also leads to death, but only rarely, and is not a direct result of epilepsy itself. This is the occurrence of a seizure during an already high-risk activity. Such activities include sky diving, race car driving, or rock climbing, in which even a momentary

People with epilepsy who engage in high-risk sports such as rock climbing face a greater risk of serious injury or death than climbers in general.

lapse of attention could result in a fatal error. The experience of a seizure while taking part in any of these activities places the individual at a very high risk of serious injury or death. For that reason, people with epilepsy must take care in choosing the types of activities in which they engage.

Epilepsy is clearly a disorder unlike any other, and no one knows this better than the people who have it. They live with the constant awareness that at any given moment they may experience something that no one else quite understands.

Chapter 2

Diagnosis and Drug Treatment

A N INDIVIDUAL HAS to meet only one condition to be diagnosed with epilepsy. He or she must have experienced two or more unprovoked seizures—that is, seizures that happened without cause. This means that even if a person has experienced ten seizures, he or she does not have epilepsy if each seizure had a specific cause, such as a traumatic head injury or a drug overdose. Similarly, a person who experiences only one random seizure also cannot be diagnosed with epilepsy. Not until a neurologist is certain that a second seizure has occurred at random is epilepsy diagnosed. As Dr. W. Allen Hauser explains, "Once a patient has a second seizure, the risk of having a third or fourth is quite high, so . . . patients should be treated [for epilepsy] after their second seizure."[6] Fortunately, most cases of epilepsy are treated successfully with a class of pharmaceuticals called antiepileptic drugs, or AEDs.

A Difficult Diagnosis

Simple as the guidelines may seem, diagnosing epilepsy is often a long and difficult process. It is not a straightforward task in which basic medical testing and examinations are all that is required. Instead, deciding whether an individual has indeed had two or more epileptic seizures is based on a thorough investigation into many areas of the patient's life. A neurologist must review the patient's medical past as well as his or her present medical condition, and a successful diagnosis requires a very strong relationship between patient and doctor. There are two reasons for this.

First and foremost is the fact that seizures themselves are very difficult to study. Because epileptic seizures strike at random and last only a short time, it is hard to catch them in the act. Therefore, neurologists rarely get a chance to witness the episodes. At all other times, the patients appear healthy. Except for seizures, there are very few clear physical or mental indications of epilepsy. This leaves neurologists little to work with during the initial diagnosis. Not only is it difficult for doctors to be sure whether their patients have experienced seizures at all, but it is also difficult to decide why those seizures occurred at all, and thus whether they are symptoms of epilepsy.

The second reason why epilepsy is so difficult to diagnose is because it is rooted in the brain. Since the brain controls the entire body, every problem the brain experiences shows itself as some form of behavioral abnormality. So, what is often thought of as an

A physician's assistant performs a neurological assessment of a patient. Diagnosing epilepsy also involves obtaining a patient's past history of seizures or injury.

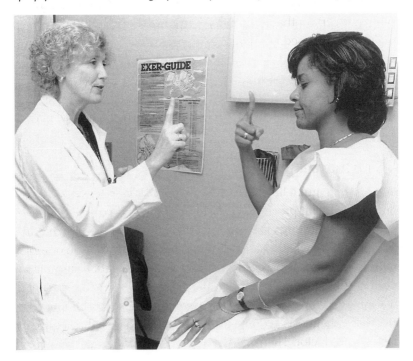

epileptic seizure is a seizure caused by something else, or it is not a seizure at all. Instead, it could be the symptom of an unrelated problem or disorder. Most people lack the medical knowledge to understand the difference, and they are often mistaken in their belief that they have experienced an epileptic seizure.

Two Paths Toward Diagnosis

Without a doubt, neurologists face a difficult task when approached by someone who may have epilepsy. The frightening seizure or seizurelike events have come and gone and left few clues behind. The events cannot be repeated on command for careful observation. This leaves two main paths for a doctor to follow in order to arrive at a diagnosis. The first is a lengthy process of communicating with the patient and those close to him or her. These talks are the only way doctors can re-create the seizurelike events, the environment in which they occurred, and the circumstances that may have caused them.

The second path, used in conjunction with the first, is to study the patient's brain itself. This is done using a group of medical tools that offer direct insight into the function and structure of the complex organ. In almost every case, a doctor is able to arrive at a correct diagnosis by combining the information gained from these two methods of diagnosis.

Patient–Doctor Communication

Every neurologist is aware that in order to make a precise diagnosis, it is vital to begin with clear, firsthand information from the patient. Doctors begin by establishing a comfortable relationship with their patients, an action that always leads to honest, detailed descriptions of what the patients have experienced. Neurologist B. J. Wilder explains: "By listening to each patient, I [can] not only arrive at diagnosis . . . but gain insight into the patient's fears, needs, expectations, self-esteem and . . . what the patient expect[s] from me."[7]

Once the lines of communication are established, there are three areas that a neurologist must investigate. First, the patient must provide the doctor with a description of the event or events that have brought him or her to the neurologist. Second, the doctor needs a description of the circumstances leading directly up to those events. Third, it is necessary to get a clear understanding of the patient's overall health and lifestyle.

The first question neurologists need to answer is whether a true seizure has occurred at all. This always involves asking the patient to explain the incident in detail: when and where it occurred, how long it lasted, and all physical and emotional feelings before, during, and after it. It is crucial that the patient do his or her best to describe the frightening incident and to verbalize any confusing and often hard-to-remember aspects of it. Because this can be very emotionally difficult, doctors must build a high level of trust with their patients. Neurologist Brien J. Smith writes that during diagnosis, "The best approach to follow in attempting to establish a successful . . . alliance is to enter the relationship with an open mind and to really listen to the patient."[8] Listening is the first step neurologists take in deciding whether their patient has indeed experienced an epileptic seizure and, if so, what type of seizure it was.

Communicating with the patient's family and friends is often another necessary step that doctors take before diagnosing

To make a clear diagnosis, neurologists often need to communicate with a patient's family and friends since individuals often have little or no memory of their seizures.

epilepsy. This is because it is common for individuals to lose consciousness during seizures and thus have little or no memory of the incident. Yet those close to the patient often witnessed the seizure, so they can complete the description and help the doctor decide what happened. In fact, when asked what things are important in order for him to diagnose someone with epilepsy, Dr. Benjamin Frishberg answered, "I need a witness!"[9]

An example of this is the story of Lucas, a seven-year-old with epilepsy. Lucas was unable to describe his first three seizures to his doctor because they all occurred while he was sleeping. However, Lucas shares a bedroom with his nine-year-old sister, and she was able to complete the picture of his seizures for his doctor. Lucas explains,

> All I remembered was feeling scared when I first woke up, because I didn't know where I was . . . and for some reason I always woke up with my arm hanging off the side of the bed. But my sister has a bed next to mine, and she told my doctor that [during the seizures] she would hear me grinding my teeth and then see only my right arm shaking for a few seconds, and fall off the bed. Then I would wake up and she would talk to me for a few minutes until I was OK.[10]

These were the neurologist's first clues that Lucas indeed had epilepsy and experienced partial seizures in the part of his brain that controls his right arm and shoulder.

Idiopathic or Symptomatic Epilepsy?

Communication between patient and doctor is not only important for deciding whether a patient has experienced true seizures. It is also crucial to discovering whether the epilepsy is idiopathic—with no known cause—or symptomatic—the result of a specific incident. This is another reason why doctors must both investigate the circumstances leading up to the incident and search for any aspects of the patient's general health and lifestyle that could result in symptomatic epilepsy.

For example, a neurologist may discover that a patient once suffered from a blood infection near the brain or recently sustained a serious head injury due to a bicycle crash in which he or she wasn't wearing a helmet. In these cases, the doctor would lean more toward a diagnosis of symptomatic epilepsy, of which both examples could be causes. On the other hand, open communication with the same patient's family may reveal that multiple relatives throughout past generations have had epilepsy, a solid hint that the patient may have idiopathic epilepsy.

Up to this point, diagnosis has resembled a puzzle. Pieces of the case have been gathered and put back together in order to form the most complete picture possible. Many times, this information is enough for the neurologist to determine whether a patient has epilepsy. Other times, however, the cause of the seizures remains a mystery. Either way, the next step is to observe both the function and structure of the patient's brain because that is where the seizures occur. Medical science has developed two amazing instruments to do this: the EEG and the MRI.

The Electroencephalogram and Magnetic Resonance Imaging

The electroencephalogram (EEG) is a tool that directly measures electrical activity within the brain. It also records that invisible activity onto paper, making it visible. The EEG is an important part of the diagnostic process because it takes these electrical measurements from separate areas of the brain at the same time. Therefore, when an EEG is finished, it has transcribed about thirty minutes of electrical activity from many areas of the brain onto paper. These separate measurements are vital because they allow neurologists to begin deciphering where in the brain any electrical abnormalities are occurring and thus understand where in the brain the seizures are focused.

By combining the results of an EEG with information gathered through communication with the patient, a neurologist is often able to diagnose epilepsy for certain. Clearly, an EEG allows the neurologist to gain valuable information about the type of seizures a patient experiences and where in the brain they occur. For example, a patient's descriptions may make it quite clear that he or she suffers from some sort of partial epileptic seizure. An

EEG may not only verify the presence of epilepsy but also clearly show where in the brain seizures are taking place, a characteristic that helps to define what type of seizures they are.

In some cases, however, the EEG still leaves unanswered questions. In such instances, doctors perform another test: magnetic resonance imaging (MRI). An MRI produces a multicolored pic-

An MRI produces a detailed image of the brain that allows doctors to study the structure of the brain and look for abnormalities that may be related to seizures.

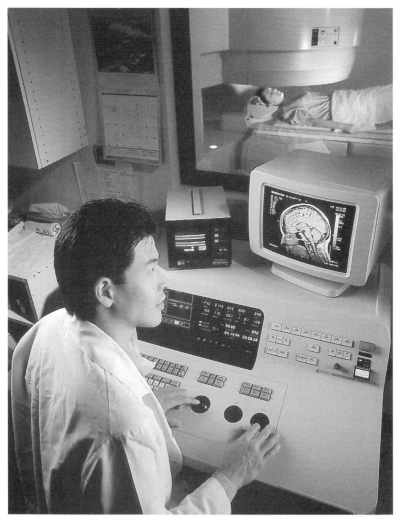

ture of the brain. This picture allows doctors to study the structure of the brain and look for damage, like tumors or scar tissue, that may be causing epilepsy (predominantly symptomatic epilepsy). If a patient experiences recurring seizures yet the results of his or her EEG are normal, an MRI may uncover the problem.

Both the EEG and MRI are incredible techniques that provide valuable insight about the human brain. However, without the patient's own ideas about his or her condition, neither test performs particularly well. Carefully studying and comparing the results of both is what allows a neurologist to determine whether a patient has epilepsy and what type of seizures he or she is experiencing. The next step is using this information to create a working treatment strategy.

Treating Epilepsy with Drugs

There is no cure for epilepsy. From the moment an individual is diagnosed with the disorder, all that his or her neurologist can do is attempt to control it. When someone with epilepsy is able to live what he or she feels is a full, satisfactory life, that person is considered to be successfully treated. For some, this means being absolutely seizure-free. For others, successful treatment means greatly reducing the number of seizures they experience, but not stopping them entirely. Either way, 80 to 85 percent of those with epilepsy discover that successful treatment includes a group of medicines called antiepileptic drugs (AEDs).

In nearly all cases of epilepsy, the first attempt to control an individual's seizures is made with one of these drugs. They are so often the starting point for treatment simply because of their long history of success. Since the first epilepsy drug was marketed in the United States in 1912, approximately twenty-six others have followed, and more are being developed. None of these drugs, however, cures the disorder. Instead, AEDs simply control epilepsy by slowing the spread of abnormal electricity in the brain, thereby reducing the number of seizures a person has.

Different types of AEDs work to control different types of seizures. Some are proven more useful at slowing the rate of generalized seizures while others are known for their ability to control

A majority of those with epilepsy can successfully treat their disorder with antiepileptic drugs.

partial seizures. Thus, when doctors discover which type of seizure is affecting their patient, they can determine which AEDs to use as treatment. Whenever possible, doctors try to treat an individual with just one AED. However, some people demand a combination of drugs for full seizure control. Either way, different people react differently to the drugs. Because of this variation in response (in addition to the variation among AEDs), finding the drug or drugs that work to treat someone successfully often takes a period of experimentation and customization. A patient may have to be put on several medications before the right one or combination is found. Nineteen-year-old Gina's experience is a good example of this. She says,

> I remember when I was thirteen and I was put on my first epilepsy medication. My three seizures a week went down to one seizure every three weeks, and we got so excited. . . . A couple months later I started having my nighttime seizures again, so my doctor increased my dosage. With that new amount [of medicine], I started losing my appetite, but not my

seizures. So we tried a new drug, first a small amount, then a little more. . . . Even after a few months I was still having two or three small seizures a week at night. . . . They were making me lose too much sleep for school. At age fourteen I tried the medicine I'm on now, and after trying two dosages I found a working plan . . . that I've been taking for the past five years.[11]

Clearly, finding an individual's best AED strategy sometimes takes a period of adjustment. However, this experimentation period does not depend only on the doctor. Because epilepsy is a condition with symptoms that strike at random, controlling the condition with medication requires a steady amount of that medicine to be in the patient's body at all times. As a result, it is very important for people with epilepsy to adhere to a strict schedule of taking their AEDs. In order to work properly, AEDs must be taken at the same time each day, sometimes up to four times a day. When the drugs don't work, the reason is commonly that the person taking them fails to understand the importance of a strict schedule.

Gary, an active twenty-four-year-old, remembers feeling weak or handicapped when he had to stop and take his pills three times a day. As he explains, "I would be out skating with my friends, and . . . skateboarding makes you feel so strong and carefree that I would skip my medicine. . . . Having to always take it made me feel like a sickly old man."[12] Adjusting and committing to changing schedules can certainly be difficult, but one of the main reasons AEDs are so successful at treating epilepsy is that they are flexible enough to match individual needs.

Side Effects of AEDs

Like all drugs, medicine for epilepsy can have both desired effects and undesired side effects. But just as different people experience different levels of seizure control with the same medication, not everyone experiences the same AED side effects. Still, there are side effects that remain common to most of these drugs. The most consistent of these are drowsiness, fatigue or sleepiness, increased clumsiness, skin rashes, and blurred vision. Some epilepsy drugs may also have more side effects in children. AEDs can affect emotions, learning and memory, and school performance. Generally,

Children may find that their learning, memory, and school performance are affected adversely when they start taking antiseizure medication. These side effects generally diminish after a treatment strategy is established.

side effects tend to be more frequent when someone is just starting to take a drug or there is a major change in the amount of a drug that is being taken. Once a treatment strategy is established, many side effects diminish in intensity or disappear altogether.

Twenty-five-year-old Amy started taking drugs to treat her epilepsy at the age of thirteen. The effects of those drugs weren't always reduced seizures, as Amy explains: "My drugs have always made living with epilepsy easier, but they've been frustrating. My mom used to have to practically stuff food in my mouth when I was younger because one of the drugs I took made me feel like I was full all the time. . . . Another made me feel like I was woozy and walking on air all the time, like the floor never felt solid underneath me." The medicines Amy takes now are a successful combination, but one of them has to be taken at night because, Amy says, "it makes me feel so out of it or unconscious that there's no way I can take it in the daytime . . . only . . . before bed."[13]

Epilepsy presents itself in a manner unlike most diseases and other disorders. The seizure, its main symptom, can happen to anyone, at any time, and for any number of reasons. This means that determining whether someone even has epilepsy demands more than just spotting the symptoms. Diagnosing epilepsy demands an in-depth understanding of many other elements related to an individual's seizures. Treating epilepsy is a similar process: There are many possibilities at first, but through work with their patients, neurologists are usually able to narrow down these possibilities and arrive at a working solution.

Chapter 3

Other Medical Treatment Strategies

APPROXIMATELY 200,000 AMERICANS have discovered that their epilepsy cannot be controlled with regular medical therapy. Even through appropriate experimentation with different types of drugs and different amounts of those drugs, some individuals find that seizures continue to interrupt their lives. Other patients find that the one drug strategy that works to control their seizures has such severe side effects it is simply not healthy. Either way, these individuals have what is called intractable, or stubborn, epilepsy, meaning that, after one full year of treatment, the patients' seizures have still not been successfully controlled.

Patients with intractable epilepsy are left with numerous options, all of which fall into two categories. One group of optional treatment strategies are those that are not supported by doctors and scientists. These strategies are called alternative treatments because they are alternatives to traditional medicine. Although some people claim that these treatments can be very helpful and effective, medical research has not proven that any of them control epileptic seizures. For that reason, neurologists and other doctors discourage their patients from relying on them.

On the other hand, the second category is made up of optional treatment strategies that have been approved by doctors and scientists. Each of these techniques has undergone rigorous testing until doctors are certain that it has a better chance of helping patients than it has of harming them. When AEDs fail them, most individuals turn to these medical treatments. Each one is more complex and involved than taking AEDs, and each one works for far fewer individuals than AEDs do. However, there are people who discover that their seizures can finally be brought under control with one of these treatments.

Modern neurology generally accepts three such treatment strategies: operating on the brain to control the seizures, stimulating the brain with electricity using a technique called vagus nerve stimulation, or putting the patient on an extremely high-fat diet called the ketogenic diet. Like the different medications for epilepsy, none of these techniques is a cure, and each works best only on certain types of seizures and individuals. Doctors maintain that an extremely thorough understanding of any case is therefore important before turning to one of these techniques.

Patients with intractable epilepsy can opt to have brain surgery, but the procedure can be risky and is not always successful.

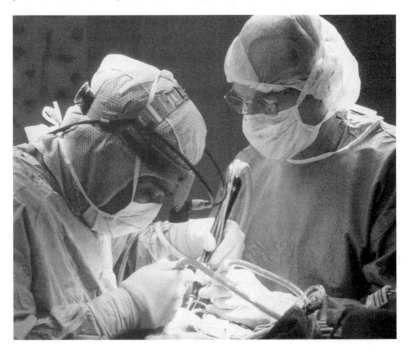

Brain Surgery

Brain surgery is a very bold step for both patients and doctors. Although it provides total control over an individual's seizures in many cases, in some instances it offers little or no relief. In addition, surgery always carries the heavy risk of interrupting the delicate manner in which the brain works. Therefore, it is not performed unless doctors are certain of a safe outcome. In fact, researchers estimate that only half of those individuals who have intractable epilepsy are candidates for brain surgery. Of the 200,000 Americans who discover each year that medications don't control their seizures, only three thousand turn to brain surgery.

When using brain surgery to treat epilepsy, there are two general strategies, and both are shaped by the same goal. In each case, doctors wish to locate precisely where in the patient's brain the seizures are occurring. This allows the neurologists to make only slight changes in the brain (the changes that are needed to control the seizures) while affecting the brain's other functions as little as possible. Because even the slightest mistake can have dire consequences, the surgeon must be very careful. As Corey Raffel,

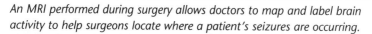

An MRI performed during surgery allows doctors to map and label brain activity to help surgeons locate where a patient's seizures are occurring.

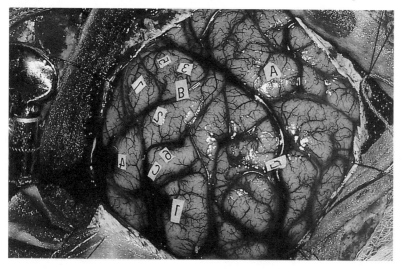

a neurosurgeon, or doctor who specializes in performing surgery on the brain, explains, "Millimeters matter here."[14]

The first and most common type of brain surgery controls only partial seizures by removing the entire area of the brain in which they take place. This strategy is called resection. The second surgical strategy is performed much less frequently. And, instead of removing brain tissue, a series of incisions are made into a specific area of the brain. These incisions stop the spread of generalized seizures. This surgery strategy is called disconnection.

Resection Surgery

On some occasions, the area of the brain in which partial seizures are located is so small and so accessible that surgeons feel it can be removed entirely without severely interrupting any other function of the brain. In these cases, resection, the surgical removal of a specific area of the brain, is performed as a treatment for epilepsy.

Even though it is uncommon overall, resection is the most frequently performed type of brain surgery for epilepsy. This is because the most common seizure is a type of partial seizure that is well understood and is often easy to locate. This seizure occurs in one of the two temporal lobes, the parts of the brain that control speech and memory. Therefore, although other areas of the brain can be removed to treat epilepsy, in 80 percent of all resection surgeries, some or all of the temporal lobe is removed to control partial seizures. This is called a temporal lobectomy.

When doctors attempt to control partial seizures with resection surgery, they strive to remove only the area in which the seizures occur. With the help of tools such as the EEG and MRI, neurosurgeons have become very skilled at this, and the success rates of resection surgeries are very high. Of patients who have all or part of their temporal lobe removed, 75 to 85 percent find that their seizures stop entirely. In addition, 90 percent of the remaining patients discover a life with a reduced number of seizures.

Additionally, because doctors are so careful before and during the procedure, problem rates are low. Only 3 to 5 percent of patients experience disturbances in those areas that are controlled by the temporal lobe, most commonly, abilities such as speaking and remembering. Finally, resection surgery has less than a 2 percent death rate.

Disconnection Surgery

Because generalized seizures spread throughout all or nearly all of the brain, it is impossible to remove only the area in which they take place. Resection surgery cannot treat this type of seizure. As a result, doctors have discovered a different technique to control some cases of generalized seizures, but they perform it much less often than resection.

Doctors have found that by making one or more very strategically placed incisions into the brain, they can sometimes disconnect the electrical paths that generalized seizures follow. Very often, generalized seizures spread across the brain horizontally, from the center out toward the sides. Therefore, a vertical cut made into the brain can create gaps that these quick side-to-side moving electrical currents can't cross, the same way that a fallen bridge stops cars traveling along a highway. Unlike resection surgery, disconnection surgery will never stop the seizures entirely. It only prevents their spread and reduces them to much less severe partial seizures.

As with resection, one type of surgery accounts for nearly all of the disconnection surgeries performed. It involves cutting the bundle of nerves that connects the two hemispheres, or halves, of the brain, thus preventing the seizures from spreading quickly from one side of the brain to the other. This form of disconnection surgery is the second most common surgery performed to treat epilepsy, after the temporal lobectomy. However, there is only an 80 percent success rate, and success means only the reduction of generalized seizures to partial seizures. Furthermore, patients often need medication afterward to maintain seizure control. The rate of complications also increases with this type of surgery, up to 15 percent. Each half of the brain controls one half of the body, and because disconnection interrupts the flow of communication from one side of the brain to the other, this surgery can lead to paralysis of one side of the body or other movement problems. Overall it is more dangerous, and thus performed less often, than resection surgery.

The Vagus Nerve Stimulator

In addition to surgery, one of the newest strategies to treat poorly controlled seizures works by emitting well-timed electrical currents into the patient's brain. This technique begins with a simple surgery that does not involve the brain in any way. Instead, doctors implant a disk-shaped device about the size of a silver dollar just below the skin on the upper left side of the patient's chest. This device, called a vagus nerve stimulator, has a thin wire connected to it that surgeons thread upward and carefully attach to a large nerve in the side of the neck called the vagus nerve. The vagus nerve is one of the many pathways of communication between the brain and the body, relaying information between the body's organs, such as the stomach, heart, lungs, and brain. In addition, it has multiple connections to areas of the brain that are often instrumental in producing seizures.

Once the device is in place, doctors program it to deliver small bursts of electrical stimulation into the vagus nerve every few minutes, around the clock. The vagus nerve then carries these electrical impulses directly to the brain, and for reasons that are still not clearly understood, these quick currents sometimes reduce seizure frequency and severity in some patients.

In addition to the device implanted in the chest, patients also carry with them at all times a small but powerful magnet that can stimulate the vagus nerve. If they feel a seizure coming on, they can wave the magnet over the stimulator implanted in their chest. This quickly produces an extra jolt of electricity into the vagus nerve, which will often prevent the seizure from happening. For that reason, this treatment strategy gives individuals a sense of personal power over their seizures the moment they occur. A magnet user named Karen says, "I have control over the monster [the seizures], it doesn't have control over me—and I can kill seizures dead with that magnet."[15] The feeling of being able to stop seizures in their tracks is an amazing and welcomed occurrence for those with epilepsy.

Because this treatment strategy has only been in use since 1997, doctors still have a lot to learn about how it works and for whom it works best. At the moment, it is clear that the vagus nerve stimulator is most effective at controlling partial seizures for epileptics over age twelve. There are fifty-eight hundred people in the United States and Europe who have been implanted with a vagus nerve stimulator, and that number is rising. Nearly all of these individuals have tried antiepileptic drugs (with un-

A doctor programs a vagus nerve stimulator for his patient, who holds an electric wand over the implant in her chest.

successful results) and were considered unsafe candidates for re-section surgery.

Although researchers do not completely understand how or why this treatment works, they do know one thing for certain: Stimulation of the vagus nerve has far fewer risks associated with it than surgery does, and far fewer side effects than AEDs. At most, patients may experience coughing, scratchiness in their speech, or slight shortness of breath. All of these side effects are the result of the stimulator and wire in the chest and neck.

Vagus nerve stimulation is clearly safe, yet it doesn't result in the amazing seizure control that brain surgery often does. General studies show that half of those using the stimulator experience at least a 20 percent daily reduction in their seizures. More than 25 percent of these individuals discover that the number of seizures they have each day is cut in half. However, there is a group of patients, about 20 percent of them, who find that their seizures increase after the device is implanted. Fortunately, it can be easily removed.

This type of treatment is clearly different from surgery: A successful outcome is less common, but overall risks are very low. For many epileptics, this means that it makes sense to try the vagus nerve stimulator. Twenty-four-year-old Erin is one such patient. She once had an average of 235 partial seizures a month and found that AEDs did not help her control them. After beginning vagus nerve stimulation, she says, "I have had 17 partial seizures on average a month. . . . I am now ready to do normal activities!"[16] Success stories such as Erin's are why each of these treatment strategies is so important, even if they don't work for everybody.

The Ketogenic Diet

Unlike surgery or stimulation of the vagus nerve, the final strategy commonly used to control intractable epilepsy does not involve medical treatment. The ketogenic diet is one in which an individual eats extremely large amounts of fatty foods, such as meat, butter, and heavy cream, and extremely small amounts of foods that are rich in carbohydrates, such as bread, cereal, and grains. This diet plan is designed to create an overall shift in the way that the human body produces energy. Traditionally, foods such as bread, crackers, and pasta, which contain carbohydrates, are the basis of what people eat each day because the human body breaks down carbohydrates and extracts energy from them. Most people try to avoid fats. The opposite is true of people on a ketogenic diet, however. This treatment strategy forces the body to break down fats in order to get energy.

Like vagus nerve stimulation, how and why this diet controls some seizures and not others remains a mystery. However, doctors are beginning to understand which individuals and which seizure types the diet treats most effectively. The ketogenic diet is successful only for children between the ages of one and ten, and it has been proven to control severe generalized seizures most effectively; it is rarely effective on partial seizures. Most often, children who find that successful drugs produce severe side effects try the diet before looking into surgery.

Several characteristics of the ketogenic diet are important to the children's parents. Most importantly, the diet has minimal side effects. Although it may produce an upset stomach and fatigue during the first few weeks, these symptoms gradually decrease as the body readjusts and learns to use its new energy sources. Some children even find that they are able to reduce their dosages of AEDs as a result of the diet's success, lessening the medicine's side effects as well. Furthermore, many parents feel they are working to control epilepsy alongside their children, a fact that gives them a greater sense of control over the disorder. Kathy, whose four-year-old son, Alex, has uncontrolled seizures, says "When I help Alex each day with this diet, I feel like his doctor as much as his mother. We're fighting this together. That's a great feeling."[17] Finally, the ketogenic diet is much less costly than all other treatment strategies.

As with all medical treatments, however, there are aspects of the ketogenic diet that make trying it a difficult decision. More than any other is the fact that it is very hard work. The diet is strict and, when done correctly, demands a lot of effort. Once the body has learned to gain its energy from fats rather than carbohydrates, even the smallest amount of excess carbohydrates can

The ketogenic diet requires patients with epilepsy to eat large quantities of fatty foods, such as meat, butter, and cheese, to force the body to break down fats instead of carbohydrates for energy.

throw the body off entirely. This means that parents have to watch their children closely and often completely change the types of food that are in the house. And if children on the ketogenic diet have brothers or sisters, it can be very hard for them to watch their siblings eat whatever they choose while they are forced to adhere to such a difficult diet.

Eight-year-old Jason used the ketogenic diet as a treatment for his epilepsy for two years (from age five to seven). His father, Steve, remembers that Jason's most difficult times on the diet were during his own birthday parties, when his friends expected to eat foods that Jason couldn't. Steve explains:

> [Jason] always wanted to have birthday cake when he had his friends over, but those kinds of desserts just can't even be tasted on this diet. It wasn't so much that he wanted the cake,

but he wanted his friends to have cake, just like they did at other parties. But we never had any cake, because we didn't want all of his friends to eat it while he couldn't. We came up with alternatives, but it was always frustrating for Jason.[18]

Despite these difficulties, the diet is worthwhile for many people who follow it. Most studies have shown that about 60 percent of all children who try the ketogenic diet discover an improvement in their seizures, at least to the point that they are able to reduce the amount of medicine they take and, consequently, the side effects that medicine causes. About half of that group are even luckier, finding that if they follow the diet carefully, it controls their seizures as well as a successful antiepileptic medication. In most cases, the diet lasts for two years and then the child is weaned off the diet and put back onto a regular diet plan over the course of a year. In some cases, children continue to experience a reduced number of seizures after such a slow transition back to a regular diet. In other cases, those finished with the ketogenic diet have better luck with AEDs. Like all treatments for epilepsy, however, the ketogenic diet does not cure the disorder. It only makes it easier to live with epilepsy.

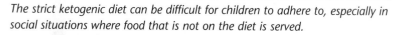

The strict ketogenic diet can be difficult for children to adhere to, especially in social situations where food that is not on the diet is served.

The group for which the ketogenic diet works is small. For that reason, the diet is not used very often. But, like brain surgery and vagus nerve stimulation, for people whose lives are improved by this treatment, it is very valuable.

In addition to AEDs, the various treatments for epilepsy (brain surgery, vagus nerve stimulation, and the ketogenic diet)—and the manner in which they control different types of seizures—reflect the complex nature of the disorder. The fact that seizures can be harnessed with such diverse treatments as a controlled diet, excess electricity in the nervous system, and surgery on the brain itself proves that epileptic seizures are connected to many aspects of human biology and warrant many complex and, as yet, unknown explanations.

Chapter 4

Living with Epilepsy

I T IS OFTEN MUCH easier for people with epilepsy to describe what life with recurring seizures is like than it is for them to describe a single episode because every seizure is different. Each one is accompanied by a different set of very personal, very confusing emotions. In addition, each is made up of a unique combination of information taken in by the senses—different sounds, scents, sights, tastes, and physical feelings. Such qualities make the experience of an epileptic seizure a difficult event to communicate.

On the other hand, the manner in which seizures shape the everyday lives of those with epilepsy is easier to express. In all cases, living with epilepsy is shaped less by seizures themselves and more by the lingering anxiety that a confusing, often embarrassing event might, at any given time, interrupt an otherwise normal existence.

As a result, when an individual with epilepsy is asked to describe a seizure in detail, answers such as nineteen-year-old Michael's are quite common: "It just seems pointless to try to fully describe one of my seizures to anyone else because I know they're never going to truly understand . . . what it's like." Yet, when asked to explain the overall meaning of epilepsy to his life, Michael is able to express his feelings using an imaginative comparison:

> Sometimes when I try to describe what having epilepsy is like to somebody who doesn't have it . . . I compare it to having the hiccups because people seem to understand that feeling of not knowing when the next little "spasm" is going to happen . . . or whether

or not another one will happen at all. They know the anxiety of focusing only on that next hiccup. When you first start hiccuping they happen one after the other, but then there might be a longer pause. . . . This is where you wonder if there will be any more. You wait and wait and wait and if it takes long enough you think they're over, but then . . . bam! Another hiccup . . . to start them back up again. I feel like if you were to spread this few minutes with the hiccups out over many years, or even a lifetime, you might get an idea of what it's like to live knowing that a string of seizures could happen at any moment.[19]

Decreasing the Burden of Epilepsy

Anxiety, embarrassment, and loss of control are some of the emotions that characterize the burden of epilepsy. The fear that a seizure may happen at any time means that, for many, living

Seizure alert dogs can ease the anxiety of not knowing when a seizure might occur.

with epilepsy is a daily challenge. Although this frustrating possibility is always present, most people are able to live normal lives because of working treatment strategies. Whether an antiepileptic drug or a successful surgery, the treatment techniques work to build a barrier against seizures, even though each strategy poses different risks for different people.

Fortunately, there is one strategy for controlling seizures that, if diligently followed, always works to increase every patient's health and happiness. This technique, which strives to create a positive lifestyle, is completely risk-free; it involves simply avoiding certain daily behaviors that are proven to place people with epilepsy at an even greater risk of seizures. Not only does this daily effort work to prevent seizures and decrease anxiety, but it also places more control of the disorder into the hands of those who have it. While other treatment strategies are outside additions to a patient's life, this plan focuses on how the patient lives his or her life. Although this strategy is less scientific and can be followed without the help of a doctor, it is something that neurologists suggest to every one of their patients with epilepsy.

For someone with epilepsy, the first step in creating a positive lifestyle is making a constant effort to avoid the many everyday circumstances that trigger seizures. Among the most common of these steps are keeping a consistent pattern of sleep, avoiding drugs and alcohol, understanding the details of one's own epilepsy, and staying free of excess stress. According to Michael, "Just like your mom tells you to sip soda instead of gulping it or eat more slowly to avoid the hiccups, there's a million things for anyone with epilepsy to do in order to avoid seizures."[20]

A Day-to-Day Rhythm

Although often overlooked, sleep is an aspect of life that truly shapes a person's daily plans, behavior, and physical condition. For people with epilepsy, sleep is so important that any sudden shifts in sleeping patterns can induce both partial and generalized seizures. In fact, sleep deprivation is such a common trigger of epileptic activity that neurologists often rely on severe lack of rest to observe a patient's seizures during diagnosis:

For people with epilepsy, getting a consistent amount of sleep is crucial in controlling seizures.

They request that the night before an EEG, a patient avoid any sleep. This increases the chance of the patient having a seizure with the EEG in place, thus allowing the neurologist to get a clear view of the seizure's characteristics. This close relationship between sleep and epilepsy can be both difficult and frustrating because sleep is one of those aspects of a person's lifestyle that affects and is affected by all other activities. Controlling it demands effort.

Going to sleep and waking up at consistent times creates a healthy rhythm that allows any brain to function at its best and avoid disruption. Those with epilepsy find that missing large amounts of sleep, or even rising early one day and late the next, can leave them feeling very vulnerable to seizures. To avoid this vulnerability, they must structure their daily pattern around this need for consistent sleep. Elements such as school or career schedules and workloads have to be organized to allow for a necessary amount of rest, usually eight hours of sleep each night. Thirty-five-year-old Linda explains how common situations, such as long airplane and automobile rides or even changes in time zones due to travel, can upset sleeping patterns and bring on a seizure:

> I travel quite a bit for business . . . not even on very long trips. But oftentimes I'm called to make a sudden one- or two-hour plane flight late at night or early in the morning for a meeting. . . . These are hours just strange enough to throw off my seven or eight hours of sleep. I don't always have seizures at these times, but when I do have seizures it's often while sitting at airport gates at hours when I would normally be in bed. . . . One of the most important things I've learned at my job is to sleep on planes or in airports, and keep my mind off of work while flying.[21]

Linda's ability to get rest in these strange places is one example of the extra effort someone with epilepsy may need to exert to prevent seizures. Such rules may seem rigorous, but the result is actually more flexibility. Instead of having to change careers or skip important traveling, Linda, like many epileptics, learned to make the necessary adaptations and now lives a full, happy life.

Avoiding Drugs and Alcohol

Alcohol and illegal drug use are other factors that pose risks to individuals with epilepsy. Like sleep deprivation, these activities are dangerous triggers of seizures and therefore must be avoided with a conscious lifestyle decision.

Every drug has a different direct effect on the brain and works to induce seizures in a different way. For example, the immediate effect of alcohol on brain function and behavior is to dull the activity of nerve cells—including neurons—until they are, in a sense, asleep. Drugs and other agents that have this effect are called depressants. For a person with epilepsy, one result of moderate to heavy drinking is that the risk of seizures increases by 50 to 60 percent. On the other hand, the illegal drug known as ecstasy has a very different effect on the brain but is still a dangerous trigger of seizures. The opposite of alcohol, ecstasy is a stimulant, meaning that it reaches the brain within forty minutes of being taken, and its toxins overexcite nerve cells. When anyone, not just epileptics, overdoses on ecstasy, one of the main symptoms is seizures or convulsions. For people who are already prone to seizures, it is even more dangerous.

The pressure to use drugs and alcohol, however, often overpowers the dangers they present. Alcohol is the most commonly abused drug in the world, and neurologists cite alcohol abuse as

Since drugs and alcohol affect the brain, people with epilepsy are advised to abstain from both.

one of the most common reasons people with otherwise controlled epilepsy between the ages of fifteen and twenty-five experience seizures. Despite their doctors' warnings, these young people ignore the risks, often because of peer pressure.

However, as they get older, many epileptics discover that the effects of alcohol and drugs on their bodies are not worth fitting in. Some even use their disorder as an excuse not to drink, and very few people can argue with the decision. Twenty-three-year-old Kendra, a college senior who has epilepsy, says,

> I've heard those statistics many times from my doctors. But that's not what's kept me from avoiding the pressures of drinking all through college. In high school I was less comfortable with letting others know I had epilepsy, and drinking was a way of proving to them that I was completely normal. . . . So I ended up partying as much as my friends. When I got to college, I learned to use my epilepsy as an important crutch. When I'm in a drinking environment with no drink in my hand and people ask why, the first thing I tell them is that I have epilepsy. . . . They immediately back off. That's what keeps me from drinking. . . . It's an amazing tool.[22]

Personal Awareness and Comfort

Stress is yet another inducer of epileptic seizures. Lifestyle skills that inhibit stress, such as confidence, organization, and necessary relaxation, are an essential part of living unhindered by the disorder, but the hectic pace of today's world often makes it difficult. Not only can excess stress result in individual seizures, but it can also start a cycle that is difficult to break. A seizure caused by anxiety or unhappiness works to intensify stressful feelings, in turn causing other seizures and more stress. "Persons with epilepsy live under a triple burden of stress," writes Adrienne Richard, an author who has epilepsy. "First, there are the stresses of daily life that affect everyone. Second, there are the anxieties of having an unpredictable symptom . . . that is misunderstood by so many people. Third, there are epilepsy's particular stressors that vary from person to person."[23]

One of the first skills neurologists teach their patients with epilepsy is to gain a detailed understanding and awareness of their disorder. Because epilepsy is an individualized condition, this awareness is slightly different for each person who has it. Doctors stress this understanding because many of them believe that when a person is familiar with the situations that trigger his or her seizures, the condition becomes more predictable and therefore less stressful.

One of the most common methods of developing this awareness is keeping a detailed journal. By recording the circumstances surrounding each seizure, patients begin to notice patterns that can add predictability to a seemingly unpredictable disorder. For example, a patient may find that seizures are more

Doctors recommend that their patients with epilepsy gain an awareness of their disorder by recording in a journal the situations that trigger their seizures.

likely to occur on weekend mornings after staying up later than usual or that seizures seem to be connected to nights of bad dreams and difficulty sleeping. When individuals can observe such patterns, they can better adapt their lifestyle to them.

Sometimes, however, patients refuse to take their doctors' advice. Recording the details of one's life in a journal first means accepting that there is a problem. This can be hard for people who feel self-conscious of or are frightened by their condition. According to twenty-two-year-old Tristen,

> My doctor urged me to keep a diary of my seizures for a long time, but I never did. I never liked the word *diary*. I lied to him and said I always wrote things down, but didn't. I felt . . . like it meant I was giving in to the seizures. Then he asked to see the journal one visit so we could look for patterns. . . . When he discovered I didn't have one, he and one of his older patients showed me the journal that patient had kept for almost five years, and the man explained to me the feeling of control it gives him when he begins to understand a certain pattern. . . . Now he knows one more situation to avoid. . . . Strange, but he said it's a feeling of power, not giving in. I've tried my best to write things down now. . . . What he said seems true.[24]

Like Tristen, many epileptics discover that uncovering those patterns can be tremendously beneficial. The story of twenty-year-old Geoff, a college student with epilepsy who experiences partial seizures, is one example of an individual who successfully uncovered a specific pattern of stressful circumstances that always seemed to lead to seizures. As a college student, Geoff learned that many of the situations that are dangerous for those with epilepsy appear together. For him, as the school semester came to a close and he began studying for final exams, the combination of anxiety, pressure to do well, upset sleeping patterns, and end-of-the-year partying almost guaranteed that he would experience seizures. Geoff says,

> I never really experienced clusters of seizures in a small amount of time until finals of my freshman year in college. I had heard stories of people staying up all night for two or three

days in a row while studying in the library, and being all stressed-out for the whole three-week period. . . . Well, it was extremely stressful, but of course I wasn't about to show any new friends . . . in the dorms that my epilepsy was any big deal. I ended up going on two all-night trips to the library with a group of friends in one week, and then sleeping until noon the days after, missing my medicine both mornings and throwing my schedule off. This, plus the stress of . . . finals, was bad enough, but add the fact that there was lots of beer around because everyone would party in their rooms immediately after a test. I went with it all, and during my third exam I had . . . four small seizures right in my seat that I tried to ignore, but I just couldn't keep writing. . . . I ended up having seven or eight more that day and then had to sleep for a day and a half straight, missing another important test.[25]

Some students with epilepsy find that the stresses of school combined with a lack of sleep can trigger a seizure.

Difficult as it was, this turned out to be a positive experience for Geoff. It was a chance to learn that, like everyone with epilepsy, his body and brain demanded a structured, orderly lifestyle regardless of outside influences. He says,

> [The] next semester I realized that finals stress is mostly in the air around finals takers. If you study alone in the day instead of all night with groups of people, things are much more relaxed. [Now] I always make finals a very alone time for myself . . . and this means explaining to people why I study alone . . . instead of hiding my epilepsy, which just causes more anxiety. . . . I also speak to . . . professors beforehand, who are always understanding. It hasn't been any sort of problem since. . . . Other students are amazed at how ahead of things I am.[26]

Individuals who attempt to avoid these seizure triggers will find themselves in a position of control. The longer seizures are avoided, the easier it becomes to prevent them from occurring at all. In addition, the confidence that comes from this daily effort makes it easier to deal with the stressful or unwelcome situations that do arise.

Facing Misconceptions

One of the most stressful and unwelcomed situations that people with epilepsy can find themselves in is actually one that doesn't involve internal stressors at all. Instead, it involves outside influences—people who misunderstand the disorder and subsequently treat those afflicted with it unfairly. Seizures can be dramatic events that are disturbing for observers, especially those who aren't educated about epilepsy. As a result, many people have little or false information to explain the confusing disorder. Epilepsy has been thought of as incredibly evil—the result of witchcraft or magic—yet it has also been hailed as heavenly— and those who have it thought of as angels. Despite the fact that modern science has proved those theories inaccurate, confusion about the disorder remains today, and people with epilepsy sometimes still face unfair treatment from others who misunderstand their condition. Part of living with epilepsy is remaining strong under such circumstances. And because epilepsy usually presents itself in childhood, this necessary strength often forms early on.

The Epilepsy Foundation of America recently compared the lives of students afflicted by epilepsy, asthma, and diabetes. These three chronic conditions have important similarities: They remain present for a long time, they restrict certain daily activities, they demand consistent medication, and they all have symptoms that may take the form of very noticeable episodes. Yet even with such similarities, researchers discovered that epilepsy affected the students' lives in a unique manner. They found that of the three groups studied, the children with epilepsy generally had the most clearly damaged self-esteem, the most problems with depression and behavior, and the most severe academic problems (these academic problems remained common even among epileptic children with normal to high intelligence levels).

A child with epilepsy plays as a nurse observes. Children with epilepsy often develop low self-esteem and have problems with depression and behavior.

When Geoff learned the results of this study, he replied,

It doesn't surprise me at all. I remember my first seizure in school in seventh grade. It seems like a small group of people had a different perception of me afterward. Some thought it was a physical problem and I felt [like an outcast] during P.E. . . . I wouldn't get picked for teams as much. Others thought [the seizure] was a sign of me being mentally retarded and thought it meant I was going to special ed classes. Whatever the case, when even a small group starts poking fun . . . it makes it easy for everyone else to join in. Reactions to that one thirty-second seizure lasted all of junior high school and even later. It doesn't surprise me that some kids with seizures have their whole school lives affected.[27]

As a result of this experience, Geoff found that, all through high school and even into college, he needed to be open about his epilepsy and try not to hide it. This honesty proved, for the most part, successful. He maintains that if he is comfortable with his condition and does his best to talk about it, others have much less of a chance of being confused and are less inclined to create misconceptions behind his back.

Adults Misunderstand, Too

Although it seems like children and teens misunderstand epilepsy most often, they are not the only ones. Adults have just as much, and sometimes more, of a problem relating to people with the disorder. "It wasn't just the kids who were confused about my epilepsy and remembered me as the 'epileptic kid' during junior high school," says Martin, a twenty-year-old recalling his early years with epilepsy. "I remember talking to teachers with my Mom, and many of them were just as lost as students when it came to understanding epilepsy and what seizures were."[28]

These misconceptions are not limited to teachers and schools. Many adults with epilepsy also experience lingering negative treatment in the workplace. In January 2000 the *British Medical Journal* published the results of a study that found that almost 20 percent of patients with seizures do not reveal the full details of

Some patients are hesitant to reveal the full truth about their seizures to their doctors for fear that it will affect their employment opportunities.

their disorders to their doctors for fear that it will affect employment opportunities. This fear is understandable considering that when a man has uncontrolled epilepsy, his probability of work is reduced by 47 percent; for women, it's 41 percent. Even for those whose seizures are completely controlled, chances of work decrease 26 percent for men and 21 percent for women. As in schools, confusion about what epilepsy is and how seizures affect people can clearly lead to discrimination in the workplace.

Aimee Copp is a basketball player for the University of Southern California who also has epilepsy and experiences consistent seizures. As a college student on the brink of adulthood, she knows the difficulties that children with epilepsy often face and is beginning to understand the boundaries that adults with epilepsy often have to cross. Despite these barriers, however, Copp has managed to maintain a place on a star basketball team, keeping up in a fast-moving sport that many would avoid if faced with uncontrolled seizures. The story of her success proves that people with epilepsy don't have to be defeated by their condition. Without a doubt, her attitude and lifestyle are what have allowed her such success. In an article about her in the *Los Angeles Times*, Copp says very simply, "If I start believing that [epilepsy] is just the way it is, just the way I'll end up, then that's what I'll do in life . . . just end up. I don't want to just end up. I want to do something." [29]

As science uncovers more and more about epilepsy, medicine will continually develop new and improved strategies to control seizures. However, an attitude like Aimee Copp's is the one treatment for epilepsy that will never change. Creating a lifestyle that allows for flexibility and options regardless of the disorder usually works for everybody. Although it is important for individuals with epilepsy to make small daily sacrifices to accomplish this, in the end these small sacrifices will prevent having to make much larger, more difficult ones in the future.

Chapter 5

The Future of Epilepsy

THE UNDERSTANDING OF epilepsy has come a long way since the Greeks first identified it. Today, doctors and scientists know that epilepsy is a complex disorder rather than a fearsome or mysterious condition. In spite of this progress, epilepsy is still far from completely understood, and basic questions remain unanswered. The reasons why some people contract epilepsy and others do not are still unclear, and science continues to be confused by the neurological abnormalities that shape seizures. This lingering confusion and incomplete understanding will remain, at least, until a cure is developed and possibly even afterward. Until then, however, researchers, doctors, and patients alike search and hope for scientific breakthroughs.

Areas of Focus

Scientists who study diseases use several key principles to guide them in their research. Through basic observation and analysis, conclusion drawing, and then controlled testing of those conclusions, they continually break new ground. Epilepsy research is no different, and each bit of information leads to new strategies for dealing with the disorder.

These strategies are focused in several areas. Some result in the development of improved techniques for diagnosis. Others lead to the possibility of better treatment strategies. Still others may result in both. However, three particular areas of research have recently demonstrated the value of different perspectives when attempting to solve a scientific mystery. They are genetic research, neural communication, and biofeedback.

A Genetic Understanding of Epilepsy

Without a doubt, the study of genetics holds the most promise for a better understanding of the basic nature of epilepsy as well as for the creation of new techniques to predict and treat it in the future. Genetics is the branch of biology that focuses on genes, tiny packets of information within cells that contain the instructions for all of the characteristics of an organism. Humans have one specific set of genes (for example, one for hair color, one for eye color, one that makes them human), some of which are the same in every person and some of which are unique. All humans are made up of tens of thousands of these genes, which are passed from parent to child.

A group of scientists, collectively known as the Human Genome Project, has been working toward creating a genetic map that shows the placement and existence of all human genes. On June 26, 2000, these scientists announced that they had created such a map. They called it the human genome, and although they had not discovered the exact role of each gene, they had pinpointed the location of each one. "We have caught the first glimpse of our own instruction book," said Francis Collins, a lead researcher in the project. "Researchers in a few years will have trouble imagining how we studied human biology without the genome sequence in front of us."[30]

For epilepsy researchers, mapping the human genome creates the possibility of uncovering the gene that controls whether a person has epilepsy. As a result, scientists are realizing that although the brain is still the stage on which epilepsy plays out its symptoms, the disorder's roots probably lie in the genetic code. As scientists become familiar with this code, the ability to alter it successfully as a means of treating—perhaps even preventing—epilepsy may not be far off.

The Value of a Genetic Understanding

Many researchers believe that being able to look at a person's genetic code and read whether he or she might develop epilepsy has several advantages. First, knowing whether an individual

A lab technician works in one of the DNA sequencing labs where scientists mapped the human genome. Researchers hope to use this code to determine which gene controls whether an individual has epilepsy.

possesses the gene for epilepsy would be an amazing tool for prediction and diagnosis. Even if a person had not yet experienced any symptoms of epilepsy, discovering that he or she did have one of these genes would be a sign that seizures might lie ahead.

With this knowledge, people would be able to prepare themselves for a life with epilepsy by learning all they could about it and planning for it with their doctors. Having the information and being able to plan for the result would allow them to be as safe and secure as possible; it would also allow them to be less frightened of the possibility of a seizure. For those already experiencing repeated but unexplained seizures, the discovery of a specific gene for epilepsy would go a long way in shortening the now lengthy and difficult diagnostic process.

Second, knowing which genes cause epilepsy would allow families with a history of epilepsy to determine who among them might be affected and, just as important, who might not. This would help alleviate the anxiety of those family members who have not yet experienced seizures but live with a fear that they might someday develop the disorder simply because it runs in their family.

Similarly, by finding out whether they have any mutant genes for epilepsy, couples planning a family would be able to make predictions about the level of risk for their future children. For example, if both future parents found that they carried the epilepsy gene, it would allow them to make important decisions, including whether they were prepared to raise a child with epilepsy (should that child develop the disorder) and whether they wanted to take the risk at all.

The final advantage, however, is the most exciting. In the future, discovery of this gene may allow scientists to develop new therapies to prevent, delay, or even reverse the onset of the disorder. Dr. W. Allen Hauser, a professor of neurology, has this to say about that exciting prospect: "Ultimately, we may . . . be able to locate the specific mechanisms that lead to epilepsy and may be able to intervene in [the process that causes it]."[31] If detailed understandings of this process were gained, doctors might be able to develop strategies to stop or reverse it. This type of treatment is called gene therapy, and it treats the disorder by altering the genes that cause it.

Gene therapy is a very difficult, complex process, yet researchers are beginning to understand it and are on the road to identifying all of the genes for epilepsy. For example, doctors have already identified a gene that is responsible for maintaining a balanced level of sugar in the blood. When this gene fails to work properly, sugar molecules build up in the blood, an event that can decrease the amount of oxygen traveling to the brain. A decrease in oxygen to the brain can destroy neurons and result in epilepsy. Each time scientists uncover new information like this, they get one step closer to designing strategies that would prevent or stop the process. Some researchers believe that in fifteen to twenty years medical treatments will be developed that can be individually tailored to a person's genetic makeup, meaning that treatments will be designed to prevent disorders like epilepsy. Researchers hope that, ten years beyond that, doctors will be able to identify and correct any genetic flaws and perhaps cure the disorder. Dr. Rochelle Hirschhorn, a professor of medicine, is certain of the value of gene therapy: "Someday people will look back on the era before gene therapy in the same way we look back on the era before antibiotics and vaccines. It is now possible to think about treating a whole series of diseases with a one-shot therapy that would last a lifetime."[32]

Discovering the Basics of Seizures

Not all research concerning the future understanding of epilepsy has strayed from the brain, however. Although progress in genetics focuses on answering the question of why epilepsy exists,

Gene therapy may allow scientists to develop new techniques to delay or even prevent the onset of epilepsy.

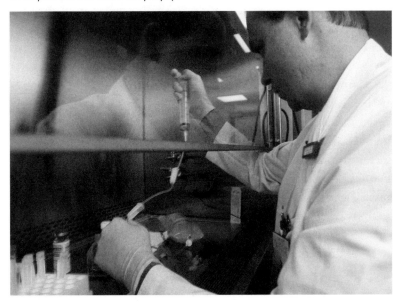

new research in neurology focuses on how epilepsy exists and how seizures occur.

Today, scientists have an incredible understanding of how neurons communicate and also how seizures disrupt that communication. Without a doubt, it is this understanding that has shaped and continues to shape much of the recent epilepsy research. Although their knowledge seems amazingly detailed, scientists continue to search, hoping to find even more minute and detailed information. They keep looking because they hope the result will be a complete understanding of exactly what abnormalities in the brain cause seizures.

When a person with epilepsy experiences a seizure, the coordinated movement of electrical messages between neurons is thrown off. One group of neurons (which should remain calm) suddenly becomes excited, communicating in a faster and more frantic manner than usual. This immediately causes surrounding neurons to do the same, and the chain reaction either remains in one area of the brain (a partial seizure) or spreads throughout the entire brain (a generalized seizure).

However, rather than studying only how large groups of neurons behave during a seizure, scientists are now researching, and beginning to understand, the behavior of each neuron during a seizure. They have begun to concentrate on the details of how electrical messages move from brain cell to brain cell and how this is altered during a seizure.

Scientists call these electrical messages spikes. Spikes travel away from a neuron along that neuron's axon, the branch connecting one neuron to another. At the spot where two neurons meet is a tiny gap called a synapse. A spike crosses the synapse to continue the electrical message, and it can only do so with the help of a special chemical called a neurotransmitter, which carries it across. The spike then enters the receiving neuron, but only in special spots that open and close in a timely manner.

Scientists are studying the coordinated action of spikes, neurotransmitters, and opening and closing neurons, each of which makes electrical communication between cells possible. It is becoming clear that the behavior of large groups of neurons (such as

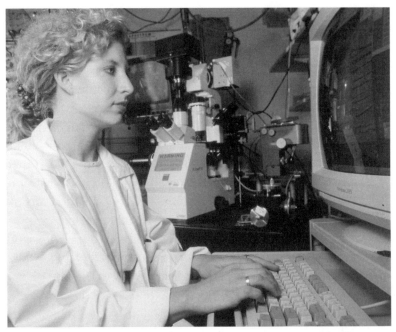

Scientists are studying the behavior of neurons in people with epilepsy in an attempt to develop a new drug that would control seizures by controlling the electrical communications between neurons.

during a seizure) is shaped by what goes on among the many neurons in that group. Therefore, learning to control these electrical communications with a drug could be one way of controlling recurring seizures. Researchers are attempting to learn all they can about the topic in the hopes of being able to develop such a drug.

New Therapies and Tools

Many doctors are confident that this understanding could revolutionize drug therapy for epilepsy. Since many of today's drugs already affect how spikes travel from neuron to neuron, a clearer understanding could lead to a drug or class of drugs that controls the process entirely. Most neurologists are certain that such drugs are a part of the future of epilepsy treatment.

As scientists attempt to gain an understanding of the basics of neuron communication, they are forced to learn new ways to observe the brain's electrical wiring. For that reason, they are also working to create new diagnostic tools. More advanced than the EEG and MRI, these tools would allow doctors to view the active brain in great detail.

One of these new diagnostic aids is the magnetoencephalogram (MEG). The MEG pinpoints sources of electrical activity in the brain by locating tiny magnetic fields that are a part of that electrical activity. Unlike the EEG or MRI, the MEG can penetrate materials such as bone and blood, and for this reason, its readings are very detailed and precise. They can also be taken by a sensor that surrounds a patient's head rather than by using more invasive tools like surgery or sensors attached to the person's body. Dr. William Sutherland, a pioneer of this technique, says, "One of the greatest advances in epilepsy surgery is non-invasive localization (MEG), where we can pinpoint the damaged tissue. The MEG can really help [patients with epilepsy]."[33]

The Power of Biofeedback

Biofeedback is a treatment technique in which people learn to take control of a bodily function over which they normally don't have control. Epileptic seizures are an example of this because neuron activity (both normal and abnormal) is a part of what science calls the involuntary nervous system. The involuntary nervous system functions without a person having to think about it at all. Thus, when it acts in a way that it shouldn't, such as during a seizure, most people believe that no one has control over it.

Using biofeedback to treat epilepsy is based on the idea that humans can, in fact, learn to control their own seizures with the help of a feedback machine. Such a technique is not new; feedback machines are a part of everyday life. For example, the heating system of a house works with feedback. When the temperature of a home's heating system is set at sixty-five to seventy degrees, sensors in the home maintain the temperature by sending signals to the heating and cooling system. If the temperature rises above seventy degrees, a signal is sent out to cool down the home. If the temperature drops below sixty-five degrees, a signal is sent to warm it up. In this way, the temperature remains at a desirable level. This is feedback.

Feedback becomes biofeedback when such a machine is used to keep one of the body's functions at a safe level. Many patients and experts are excited about it as a possibility for controlling seizures. According to Dr. José Chaves, "Biofeedback stands out as one of the most revolutionary and promising approaches to

Biofeedback is gaining popularity as a risk-free treatment for controlling seizures.

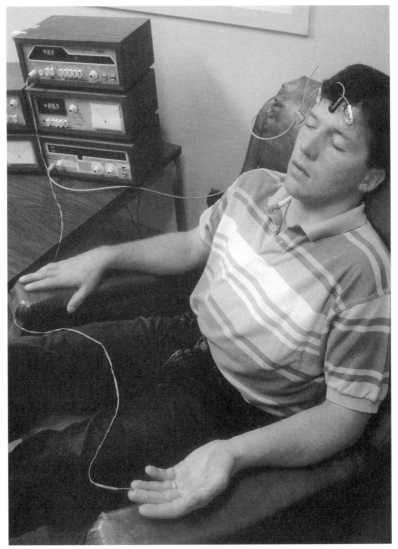

[treating epilepsy], and . . . can be considered one of the therapies most likely to prevail in the 21st century."[34]

Biofeedback systems that treat epilepsy use electronic sensors to measure brain electricity levels. Much like an EEG, these sensors are connected to the scalp and take readings of brain activity levels. The readings go directly to a computer monitor that then displays them in the form of a continuous graph. As a result, the patient has the chance to witness the way in which his or her behavior is affected by brain electricity. This visible information gives the patient the opportunity to compare the feeling of a seizure, which he or she knows well, with the electrical excitability in his or her brain that accompanies it. The goal is for those with epilepsy to work with this system a number of times each week and to become familiar with behaviors that help them calm their brain electricity. In this way, they can learn techniques to offset dangerous patterns that emerge and to ultimately relax the excited neurons on their own. By using techniques such as deep breathing, calm thoughts, and meditation, doctors contend that many people can eventually learn to control their epilepsy without the biofeedback system at all.

Experts have been mastering this system for the past eight to ten years, and it is now used to treat some cases of epilepsy in the United States, Japan, Canada, France, and Brazil. Thousands of articles in medical journals have documented its possibilities, and thousands of experts worldwide use it to treat their patients. Biofeedback is an exciting prospect for the future because of its lack of risks and side effects and because of the sense of accomplishment it leaves with anyone who masters it.

Martha, a thirty-eight-year-old woman who has experienced partial seizures since her teen years, can't imagine biofeedback not catching on in the coming years: "All the other treatments I've tried . . . mostly AEDs, have been a 'try' then 'wait' game, over and over. Just wait and see if it works, over and over. The idea of feedback makes such perfect sense. . . . I think once people learn to trust a technique that's a little different . . . it will become extremely popular."[35]

Progress toward a complete understanding of epilepsy in the future clearly relies on viewing the disorder from many angles.

The work being done now is proof that solving a complex puzzle like epilepsy demands using pieces from all areas. Although it is evident that the roots of the disorder may lie in human genetic information, it is also obvious that the mystery of epileptic seizures will be solved only through detailed research into the activity of brain cells. Each of these possibilities is important to the future of epilepsy.

Notes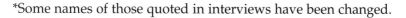

*Some names of those quoted in interviews have been changed.

Introduction: A Temporary Loss of Control
1. Nigel, interview by author, Cardiff-by-the-Sea, California, March 22, 2000.

Chapter 1: What Is Epilepsy?
2. Matt Walker, "Just Slow Down," *New Scientist*, September 18, 1999, p. 16.
3. Steven, interview by author, Cardiff-by-the-Sea, California, September 20, 1999.
4. Elana, interview by author, Cardiff-by-the-Sea, California, February 11, 2000.
5. Mark, interview by author, University of California, Berkeley, March 2, 2000.

Chapter 2: Diagnosis and Drug Treatment
6. Quoted in Doctor's Guide to Medical and Other News, "Researchers Establish Parameters in Epilepsy Diagnosis," February 12, 1998. www.pslgroup.com/dg/SADB6.htm.
7. Quoted in Steven C. Schachter and A. James Rowan, eds., *The Brainstorms Healer: Epilepsy in Our Experience: Stories of Health Care Professionals as Care Providers and Patients*. Philadelphia: Lippincott-Raven, 1998, p. xvi.
8. Quoted in Schachter and Rowan, *The Brainstorms Healer*, p. xxvii.
9. Benjamin Frishberg, interview by author, Scripps Hospital, Encinitas, California, November 2, 1999.
10. Lucas, interview by author, Oceanside, California, April 27, 2000.

11. Gina, interview by author, University of California, Berkeley, March 3, 2000.
12. Gary, interview by author, San Francisco, September 1, 1999.
13. Amy, interview by author, Cardiff-by-the-Sea, California, August 12, 1999.

Chapter 3: Other Medical Treatment Strategies

14. Quoted in Jill Burcum, "Thanks to Mayo, a Chance to Be Seizure-Free and Normal Again," *Minneapolis Star Tribune*, December 4, 1998, p. 1B.
15. Quoted in Cyberonics, "Profiles in Courage" (company literature), Houston, 1999.
16. Quoted in Cyberonics, "Profiles in Courage."
17. Kathy, interview by author, Oceanside, California, April 2, 2000.
18. Steve, email to the author, May 3, 2000.

Chapter 4: Living with Epilepsy

19. Michael, interview by author, Solana Beach, California, August 10, 1999.
20. Michael, interview by author.
21. Linda, interview by author, San Diego, California, April 14, 2000.
22. Kendra, interview by author, San Diego, California, April 14, 2000.
23. Adrienne Richard and Joel Reiter, *Epilepsy: A New Approach.* New York: Prentice-Hall, 1990, p. 138.
24. Tristen, interview by author, University of California, San Diego, May 4, 2000.
25. Geoff, interview by author, Berkeley, California, September 3, 1999.
26. Geoff, interview by author.
27. Geoff, interview by author.
28. Martin, interview by author, Oceanside, California, November 12, 1999.
29. Quoted in Bill Plaschke, "USC's Copp Unshaken in Resolve to Combat Epilepsy," *Los Angeles Times,* February 11, 1999, p. D-1.

Chapter 5: The Future of Epilepsy

30. Quoted in Seth Borenstein, "Breakthrough Deciphers the Very Language of Life," *San Diego Union-Tribune*, June 27, 2000, p. A-1.

31. Quoted in Lynne Christenson, "Genetics and Epilepsy," *P&S Journal*, Fall 1995. http:// cpmcnet.columbia.edu/news/journal/archives/jour_v15n3_0009.html.

32. Quoted in March of Dimes, "Genetic Testing and Gene Therapy: What They Mean to You and Your Family," June 17, 2000. www.noah.cuny.edu/pregnancy/march_of_dimes/genetics/genetest.html.

33. Quoted in Neurosciences, "Epilepsy Technology," 1995. www.goodsam.org/press/library/neuro/EPILTECH.html.

34. José Chaves, "Biofeedback: The Therapy of the Twenty-First Century," Group of Electronic Publications in Medicine, Biology, and Health, August 6, 1999. www.epub.org.br/cm/n04/tecnologia/biofeed_i.htm.

35. Martha, telephone interview by author, June 12, 2000.

Glossary

antiepileptic drug (AED): A pharmaceutical developed to control the occurrence of epileptic seizures.

axon: The single extension of a neuron that conducts electrical impulses away from the cell body.

biofeedback: A technique for treating a disease or disorder based on an individual's control of bodily functions that are normally automatic.

chromosome: One of the rod-shaped bodies in the nucleus of a cell that contains the organism's genetic material, or DNA.

convulsion: A common term for the tonic-clonic generalized seizure that involves the repeated tightening of muscles and jerking of limbs.

deoxyribonucleic acid (DNA): The complex molecule present in every living cell consisting of chemical subunits that determine an organism's genetic makeup.

depressant: A drug such as alcohol that dulls or slows the action of neurons in the brain.

diagnosis: The identification of a disease or disorder by its characteristic symptoms.

disconnection: A surgical treatment for epilepsy that involves making incisions into the brain to stop the spread of generalized seizures.

electroencephalogram (EEG): A machine that records the electrical activity of the brain.

focus: The area of the brain in which a seizure takes place or originates.

gene: A chemical unit positioned on the DNA molecule that transmits a specific biological trait from parent to offspring.

generalized seizure: One of two groups of epileptic seizures; generalized seizures spread throughout the entire brain rather than remaining focused in one area.

gene therapy: An approach to treating certain disorders that is based on the modification of an individual's genes.

genetics: The branch of biology that deals with heredity and variation among organisms.

genome: The complete genetic code of one person.

hypothesis: An educated guess or assumption made about a situation, based on earlier understanding and analysis.

idiopathic epilepsy: Epilepsy of an unknown cause.

intractable epilepsy: Epilepsy that cannot be controlled with antiepileptic drugs.

ketogenic diet: A high-fat, low-carbohydrate diet that forces the body to derive energy from fat; for unknown reasons it controls generalized seizures in some children.

magnetic resonance imaging (MRI): A diagnostic tool that uses magnets and sound waves to collect detailed images of the structure of the brain.

neurology: The branch of medicine concerned with the brain and nervous system.

neuron: A cell of the brain and nervous system specialized to transmit information in the form of tiny electric impulses.

neurotransmitter: A chemical that carries electrical impulses across the gap between neurons.

partial seizure: A seizure that remains localized in the area of the brain from which it originated.

resection: A surgical treatment for epilepsy that involves removing the area of the brain in which partial seizures are focused.

seizure: A sudden discharge of excess electricity within the brain that causes a momentary shift in behavior.

spike: A single electrical impulse sent from one neuron to another.

status epilepticus: A life-threatening condition characterized by either a prolonged seizure or a series of quickly repeating seizures.

stimulant: A drug that increases the activity of the brain and brain cells.

stroke: The sudden blockage of blood circulation to the brain or part of the brain; can result in epilepsy.

symptomatic epilepsy: Epilepsy resulting from a known cause.

synapse: The gap that lies between the axon of one neuron and the next neuron.

temporal lobe: The area of the brain that controls memory; most common site of partial seizures.

temporal lobectomy: The surgical removal of all or part of the temporal lobe to control partial seizures focused there.

vagus nerve: The large nerve in the neck; it acts as a pathway for information traveling between the brain and other large organs, such as the heart and lungs.

vagus nerve stimulator: A treatment for epilepsy that controls seizures with small jolts of electricity delivered into the brain via the vagus nerve.

Organizations to Contact

American Epilepsy Society (AES)
342 N. Main St.
West Hartford, CT 06117-2507
(860) 586-7505
website: www.aesnet.com

This organization promotes research and education for people interested in and dedicated to the prevention of epilepsy. The AES stays abreast of all breakthroughs in the areas of epilepsy treatment and diagnosis.

Epilepsy Education Association
4335 1C Irish Hills Dr.
South Bend, IN 46614-3110
(219) 273-4050
website: www.iupui.edu/epilepsy/

This group focuses on increasing the public's understanding of epilepsy and clarifying misconceptions. It offers programs directed toward patients, families, the public, and physicians. It emphasizes lifestyle progress for the patient with intractable epilepsy.

Epilepsy Foundation of America (EFA)
4351 Garden City Dr.
Landover, MD 20785
(301) 459-3700
website: www.efa.org

This organization represents the interests of people with epilepsy through the services of its eighty local affiliates. These services include parent and patient information, counseling and referrals, employment assistance, and medical advice. The EFA also coordinates statewide resources for those with epilepsy.

Epilepsy Foundation of New York City
305 Seventh Ave.
New York, NY 10001
(212) 635-2930
website: www.efnyc.com

Founded in 1971 as a nonprofit organization, the aim of this group is to help individuals evaluate and understand the most important medical, social, and personal issues associated with epilepsy.

Epilepsy Ontario
1 Promenade Circle, Suite 308
Thornhill, ON L4J 4P8
CANADA
(905) 764-5099
website: www.epilepsyontario.org

This group aims to improve the quality of life for all people with epilepsy with services for both children and adults. Standout events include Spike and Wave summer camp for kids with epilepsy, Epilepsy Awareness, and the GLAD Days celebration. All funding is from the public.

For Further Reading

Books

Rachel Anderson, *Black Water*. Baltimore: PaperStar Books, 1996. This book offers a historical view of the disorder and is written for children. It follows a young boy with the so-called falling sickness in nineteenth-century England.

Sally Fletcher, *The Challenge of Epilepsy*. Santa Rosa, CA: Aura, 1985. An easy-to-read guide meant to instruct, encourage, and inspire people with epilepsy. The author has epilepsy herself, and she claims to have created her own set of solutions to defeat it.

Susan Dudley Gold and Mark E. Dudley, *Epilepsy*. New York: Crestwood House, 1997. This presentation of the disorder is geared for nine- to twelve-year-olds.

Elaine Landau, *Epilepsy*. New York: Twenty-First Century Books, 1994. This book is a very basic introduction to the disorder and is written for young readers. It covers basic topics such as seizure definition and descriptions.

Alvin and Virginia Silverstein, *World of the Brain*. New York: William Morrow, 1986. Simplified introduction to the brain's amazing abilities and its role in everyday behavior. The authors have written numerous books covering science and natural history for young adult readers.

Andrew N. Wilner, *Epilepsy: 199 Answers: A Doctor Responds to His Patients' Questions*. Boston: Demos Medical, 1996. An encyclopedic reference of the disorder, from basic questions and confusion to more complex, personal issues. This book is valuable for people with and without epilepsy as well as for all age groups.

Periodicals

Kathryn S. Brown, "Mending Broken Genes," *Popular Science*, October 1999.

Ezra Hodge, "Teen Takes on Epilepsy," *Times-Picayune*, March 18, 1999.

Chris O'Malley, "Biology Computes," *Popular Science*, March 1999.

Chrissy Ruggiero, "My Walk with Epilepsy," *Houston Chronicle*, November 19, 1998.

Websites

EpiCentre (http://ourworld.compuserve.com). This is a comprehensive introductory site that covers all of the basics of epilepsy, from definitions to causes to treatment. Graphics are well done and attention grabbing.

Epilepsy Foundation of America (www.efa.org). This is the largest epilepsy group in the nation, and it has an amazing website that is perfect for the browsing learner. Topics covered include personal perspectives on epilepsy, modern research, and the latest treatment breakthroughs. It also offers important links to other epilepsy-related groups.

Excite Health (www.03excite.com). A valuable starting point for people interested in the disorder. Its easy-to-follow information about the brain and nervous system lead smoothly into epilepsy and related issues.

KidsHealth (http://kidshealth.org/kid/health-problems/epilepsy.html). This site offers "An Epilepsy Education," which is the perfect starting point for eight- to twelve-year-olds interested in epilepsy. Its easy-to-follow format focuses on the basics of the disorder while stressing the idea that people with epilepsy can and do lead fully functional lives.

ThriveOnline (www.thriveonline.com). This site is excellent for research because of a continually updated list of documents, articles, and essays concerning epilepsy. Contributing authors are from all over the world.

Works Consulted

Books

Thomas R. Browne and Gregory L. Holmes, *Handbook of Epilepsy.* New York: Lippincott-Raven, 1997. A pocket-size "handbook" composed of clear clinical reviews covering all areas of management and diagnosis of epilepsy. This book targets practitioners but is readable by laypeople.

Sudhansu Chokroverty, *Management of Epilepsy.* Boston: Butterworth-Heinemann, 1996. A step-by-step guide to managing patients with all types of epilepsy. It covers seizure types, different syndromes, and specific problem-oriented situations. It is geared toward the nonspecialist.

John M. Freeman, Eileen P. G. Vining, and Diana J. Pillas, *Seizures and Epilepsy in Childhood: A Guide for Parents.* Baltimore: Johns Hopkins University Press, 1990. This book is written specifically for the parents of children with epilepsy. It combines information on basic topics, such as diagnosis and treatment, with advice and support for parents learning about the disorder as their children deal with it.

James W. Kalat, *Biological Psychology.* New York: Brooks/Cole, 1995. This college textbook focuses on the connection between human behavior and neural anatomy. It is an excellent reference for understanding how the biology behind a seizure results in the physical display that it does.

Arthur M. Lassek Sr., *The Unique Legacy of Doctor Hughlings Jackson.* Springfield, IL: Charles C. Thomas, 1970. A biography of Hughlings Jackson (1835–1911), the pioneering epileptologist who began formulating the concepts and principles that ultimately led to the definitions of many seizure types.

Wilder Penfield and Herbert Jasper, *Epilepsy and the Functional Anatomy of the Human Brain.* Boston: Little, Brown, 1954. This book offers a detailed overview of epilepsy's relationship to the working brain. Penfield, who revolutionized certain brain-surgery techniques and made key discoveries about human cognition, has valuable insight.

Adrienne Richard and Joel Reiter, *Epilepsy: A New Approach.* New York: Prentice Hall, 1990. This guide is the collaboration between a writer with epilepsy and a well-known neurologist. It combines the insight of an individual who has overcome epilepsy without powerful drugs and that of a physician who had made critical advancements in our understanding of the disorder.

Maria A. Ron and Anthony S. Davis, eds., *Disorders of Brain and Mind.* New York: Cambridge University Press, 1998. With the help of the different insights of twenty-two contributors, the editors have put together a detailed introduction to both the physical and behavioral aspects of most neurological disorders.

Steven C. Schachter and A. James Rowan, eds., *The Brainstorms Healer: Epilepsy in Our Experience: Stories of Health Care Professionals as Care Providers and Patients.* Philadelphia: Lippincott-Raven, 1998. One of a four-part series by Dr. Schachter called the Brainstorms Series. Each offers insight into a different area of living with the condition, with the contributions of both scientists and everyday individuals with epilepsy.

Michael Shaw, ed., *Everything You Need to Know About Medical Tests.* Springhouse, PA: Springhouse, 1996. Seventy leading specialists have contributed to this book. It covers many concerns about all types of medical tests, including why and when they are performed, what happens, and what abnormal results mean.

William S. Svoboda, *Learning About Epilepsy.* Baltimore: University Park Press, 1979. This introductory text highlights differences in the terminology and general understanding of epilepsy as well as the progress continually being made in treatment and diagnosis.

Paul Thagard, *How Scientists Explain Disease*. Princeton, NJ: Princeton University Press, 1999. Thagard analyzes how disease mechanisms are discovered, explained, and accepted. In addition to basic science, he focuses on the mind, society, and experimentation as equally important factors in the development of new theories.

Owsei Tomkin, *The Falling Sickness: A History of Epilepsy from the Greeks to the Beginnings of Modern Neurology*. Baltimore: Johns Hopkins University Press, 1971. This book provides thorough coverage of the unique role that epilepsy has played throughout history in the scientific and unscientific communities. Relates prejudices against people with epilepsy and the cultural barriers that are set up against those studying the disorder.

Charles P. Warlow and Jan Vana Gijn, *Stroke: A Practical Guide to Management*. Boston: Blackwell Science, 1996. This book offers an overview of the popular procedures followed during the diagnosis and management of strokes. It reviews the causes, types, and biological effects of strokes, including epilepsy.

Lawrence M. Way, *Current Surgical Diagnosis and Treatment*. Norwalk, CT: Appleton & Lange, 1994. This is a review of one thousand diseases and disorders based on diagnosis and treatment. It emphasizes cost-effective care, outpatient surgical techniques, and ambulatory care.

Periodicals

Hasan Aziz, Syed Wasim Akhtar, and K. Kaki Hasan, "Epilepsy in Pakistan: Stigma and Psychosocial Problems," *Epilepsia*, October 1997.

Seth Bornstein, "Breakthrough Deciphers the Very Language of Life," *San Diego Union-Tribune*, June 27, 2000.

Jill Burcum, "Thanks to Mayo, a Chance to Be Seizure-Free and Normal Again," *Minneapolis Star Tribune*, December 4, 1998.

Lynne Christenson, "Genetics and Epilepsy," *P&S Journal*, Fall 1995.

Rex Dalton, "Fetal Pig Cells as Epilepsy Therapy Studied," *San Diego Union-Tribune*, December 8, 1998.

Susan Ferraro, "Implant Can Change the Lives of Epileptics," *New York Daily News*, January 25, 1999.

Jack Innis, "Ocean Rower Halsey OK After Second False Alarm," *Log*, January 14, 2000.

Scott LaFee, "A Brain Besieged," *San Diego Union-Tribune*, November 17, 1999.

Michael Lasalandra, "Gene Find May Bring Epilepsy Advances," *Boston Herald*, December 23, 1998.

Bill Plaschke, "USC's Copp Unshaken in Resolve to Combat Epilepsy," *Los Angeles Times*, February 11, 1999.

Matt Walker, "Just Slow Down," *New Scientist*, September 18, 1999.

Internet Sources

José Chaves, "Biofeedback: The Therapy of the Twenty-First Century," Group of Electronic Publishers in Medicine, Biology, and Health, August 6, 1999. www.epub.org.br/cm/n04/tecnologia/biofeed_i.htm.

Doctor's Guide to Medical and Other News, "Researchers Establish Parameters in Epilepsy Diagnosis," February 12, 1998. www.pslgroup.com/dg/SADBG.htm.

March of Dimes, "Genetic Testing and Gene Therapy: What They Mean to You and Your Family," June 17, 2000. www.noah.cuny.edu/pregnancy/march_of_dimes/genetics/genetest.html.

Neurosciences, "Epilepsy Technology," 1995. www.goodsam.org/press/library/neuro/EPILTECH.html.

Other

Cyberonics, "Profiles in Courage" (company literature), Houston, 1999.

Index

Picture Credits

About the Author

Twenty-six-year-old Gregory Goodfellow began writing and editing after earning his bachelor's degree from the University of California at Berkeley. Much of his work has been targeted toward younger audiences, from his associate editor position at a popular action sports/lifestyle magazine to his freelance work for numerous websites that also focus on elements of youth culture. Goodfellow has epilepsy himself, and he enjoys sharing the experience by writing for epilepsy support groups and organizations as well as by being a Big Brother to children with the disorder. Goodfellow lives in Cardiff-by-the-Sea, California, and he is presently a reporter/writer for *Midrange Computing* magazine. *Epilepsy* is his first book.